MADE FOR OUR FAMILY

The Big Surprise!

KimFord

Relevant Publishers LLC

SUTTON, ALASKA

Becoming Noonie

When I was a kid I couldn't imagine ever being a grandma. I never thought I'd be that old!

But I grew up, got married, and had kids, and then my kids grew up, got married, and had kids of their own.

Grandmothers have many special names, like Nana, Lolli, Gigi, or Grammy, but my grandma name is "Noonie." It sounds funny, but I love it! I tried to pick a different name, "Nona," but when my granddaughter was little, she couldn't say it right and said "Noonie" instead. Now I have seven grandkids. I love each grandchild so much. Maybe there will be more grandkids one day, and that would be amazing. But for now, I want to tell you the birth stories of my seven wonderful grandkids.

You may wonder how babies come into the world and what it's like to be a big brother or sister. Every child has their own special story about how they joined their family and how they got their name. If a new baby is coming to your family, I hope these stories help you get ready for the big day!

Dear Parents:

This book is written to help you teach your child about the sanctity of human life and to open up conversation about their own birth story. If you want to share with them their unique story from even before they were born, this is a great time to do so. All children love hearing about how they came into their own family.

Maybe you have the sonogram photos from your child's ultrasound and can show them what they looked like when they were a pre-born baby. Or, maybe you are pregnant and have your next ultrasound scheduled. This might be a perfect opportunity to help your child learn about the early beginnings of life and to also bond with their soon-to-be brother or sister.

Treasure this precious time with them when they are young. It goes by all too fast, as those older folks in the grocery store like to tell you as you wait in line at the check-out stand. It's really true.

Bless you as you raise your littles!

Love,
"Noonie"

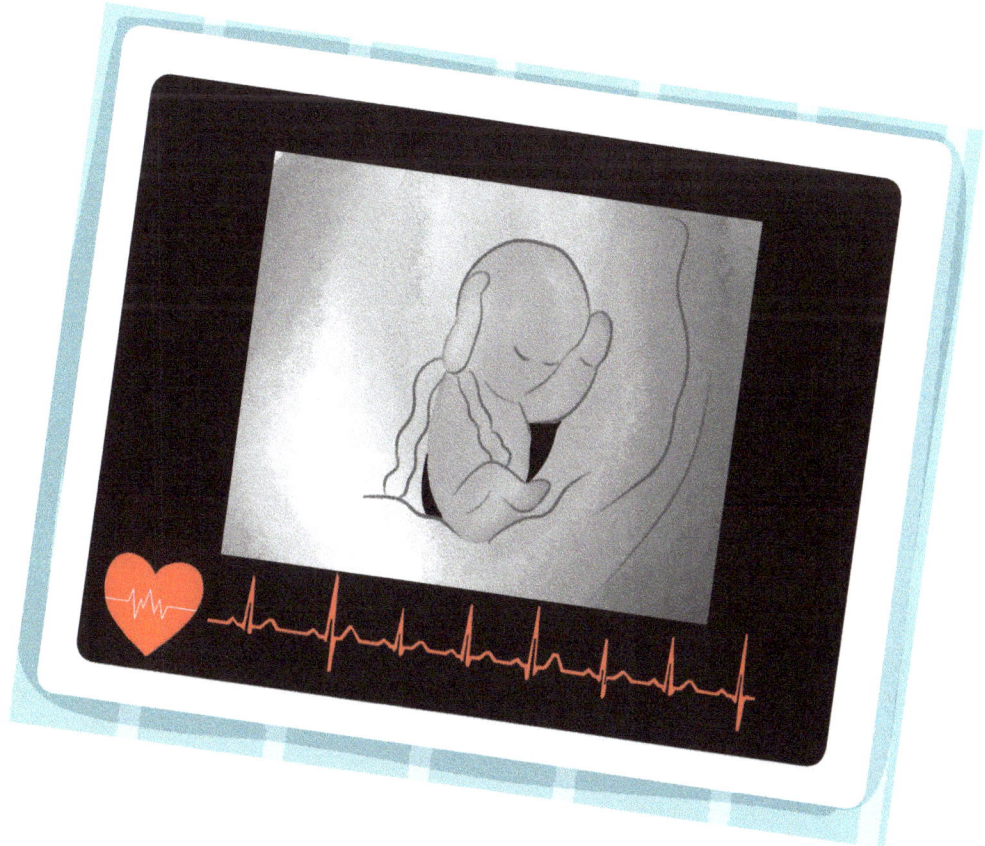

One special day we got a phone call from our daughter and son-in-law. They had BIG news to tell us! They were expecting a baby!

ALASKA

WYOMING

We were so excited to be grandparents! We wanted to tell everyone the good news, but they asked us to wait for the right time before telling anyone.

They wanted to wait until after they went to the doctor and had an **ultrasound**.

This is an amazing machine that uses sound waves to form pictures on a TV screen so we can see what is in a mama's belly!

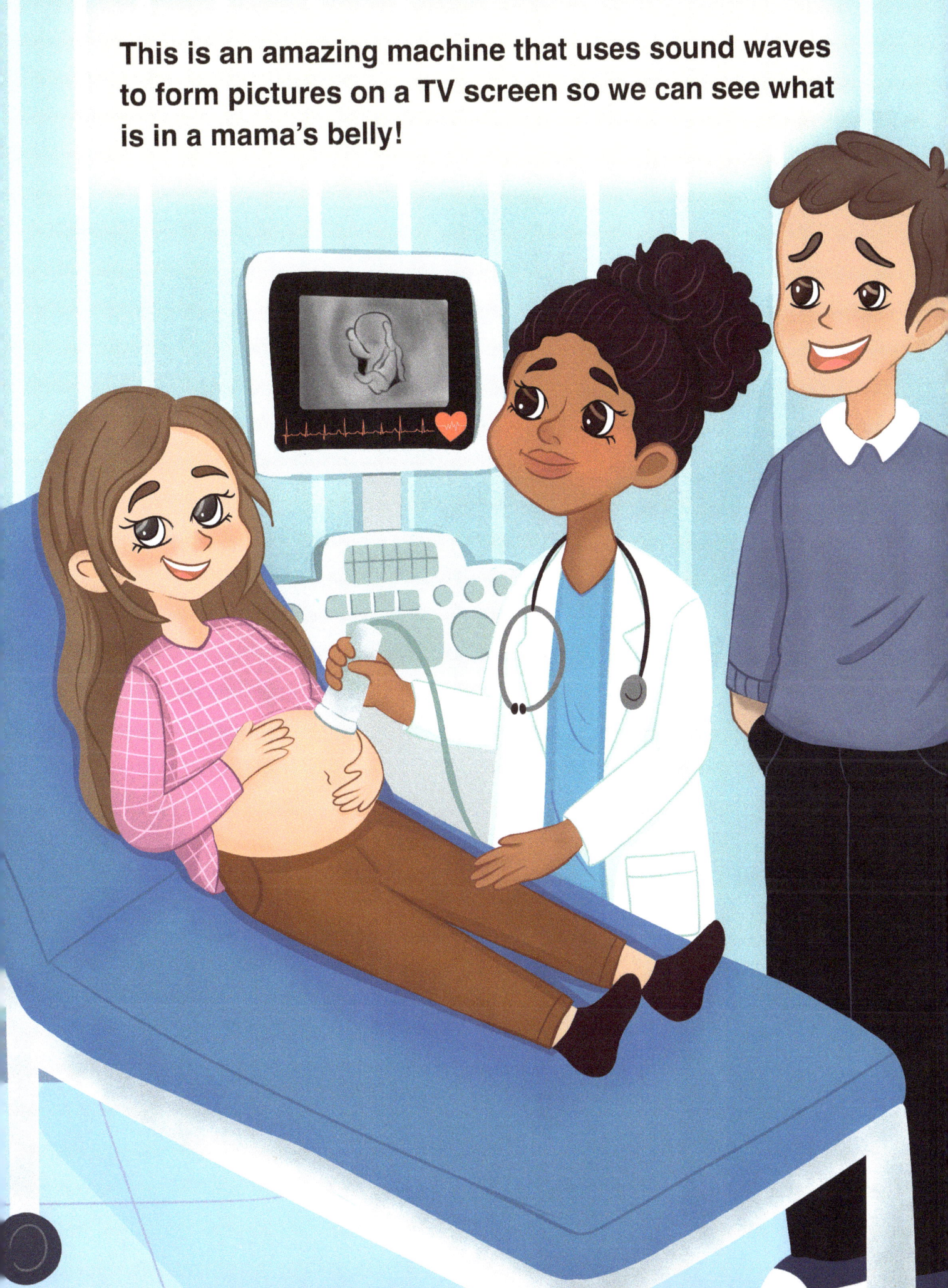

Some of the information they find out from the ultrasound tells them when the due date will be for the baby to be born,

how many babies are in the womb,
1 or 2,

and if it is a boy or a girl.

The coolest thing about an ultrasound is that you get to watch the baby in the womb as it moves around.

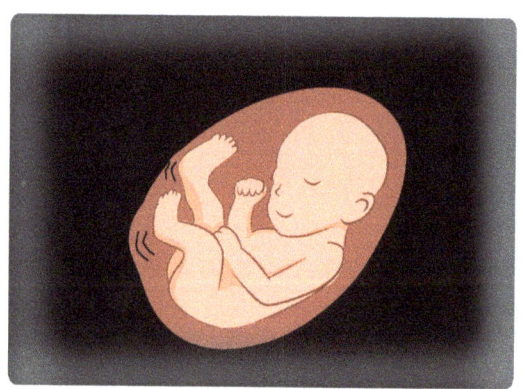 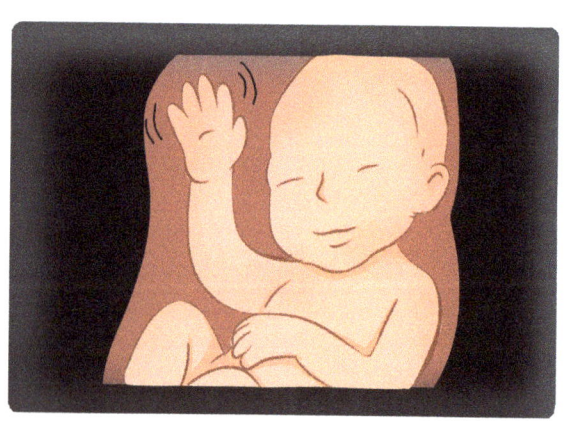

Babies kick, do flips, and wave.

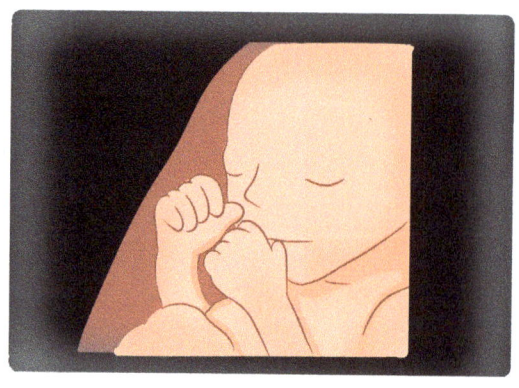

Sometimes they even suck their thumb!

A baby in the womb can hear sounds going on inside and outside the mama's belly, like the mama's singing, the baby's dad talking nearby, or a dog barking!

Did you know that a baby can even taste the foods the mother eats while she is pregnant?

What foods taste yummy or yucky to you?

Pregnancy is broken up into three stages: the first, second, and third **trimesters**. One cool thing that happens in the first trimester is the baby's heart begins to beat.

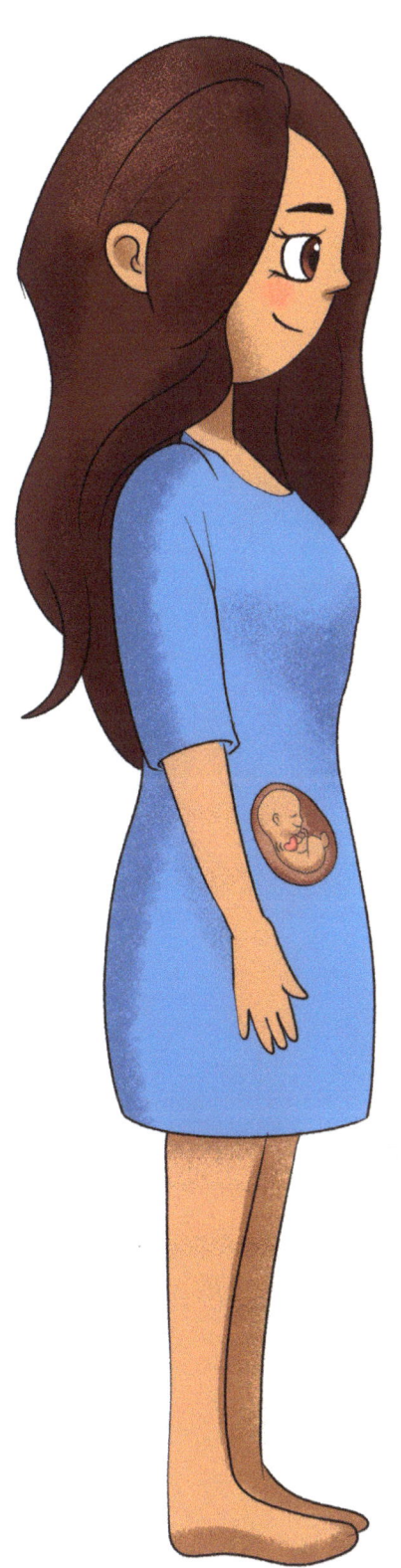

• A baby's heart can beat up to 170 beats per minute, twice as fast as the mom's.

• All major organs are forming.

• Arms and legs are growing.

• The umbilical cord is formed. This is how food travels from the mama's body to her baby in the womb.

First Trimester

Sometimes in the first trimester mamas can feel very sick to their stomach. It's called "morning sickness," but most of the time it lasts all day for quite a while.

To help with this your mom might eat a lot of small snacks more often than you are used to seeing. But don't worry…you don't need to eat as often as she does. She is feeding herself AND the baby inside.

In the second trimester, the baby is growing bigger and developing all it's systems...like for eating, thinking, and moving. The baby is the size of a tiny pumpkin.

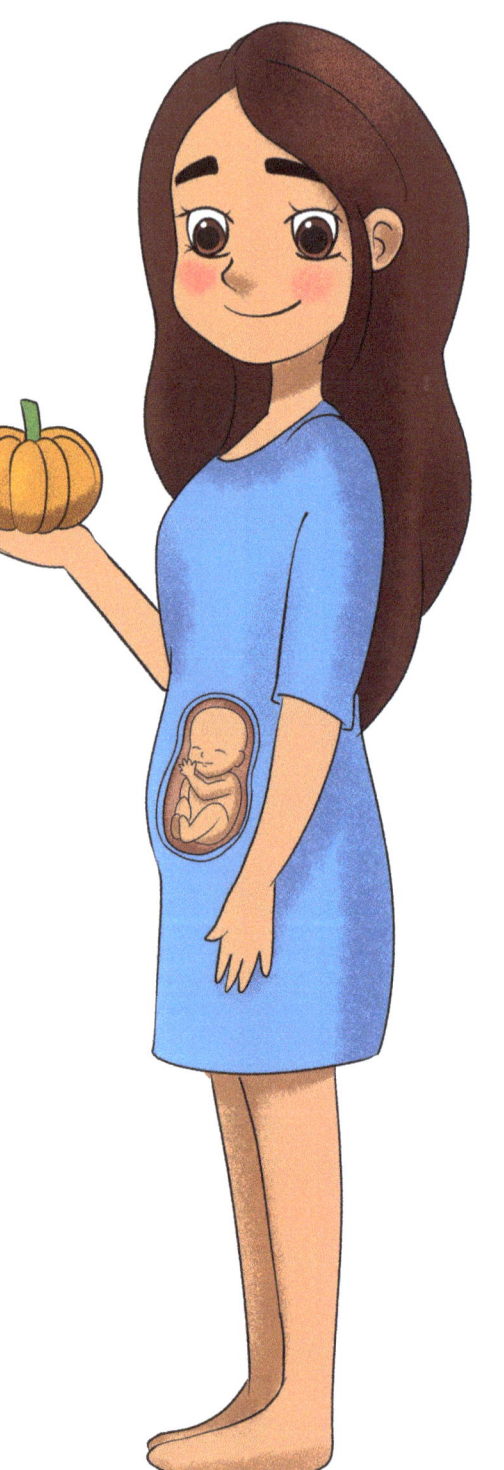

- Facial features are formed

- Fingerprints are developed

- Digestive System is functional

- Brain is growing

- They can make expressions that are seen on an ultrasound

Second Trimester

In the third trimester, the baby is fully formed and mainly just growing bigger until the day arrives to be born.

- Baby is the size of a small pumpkin

- Baby is ready to live outside its mama's belly in the final month of pregnancy

Third Trimester

When my daughter got to the end of her third trimester, I flew from Alaska to Wyoming to be there for the birth. I was so excited to be there to meet my grandson!

Well baby Paul was in no rush to come out from his mama's belly where he was cozy and safe. We did a lot of waiting…

What would you do if you had to wait for a baby to be born and it was past its due date?

Finally the day arrived for baby Paul to be born! We were so glad to be heading to the hospital for his birth.

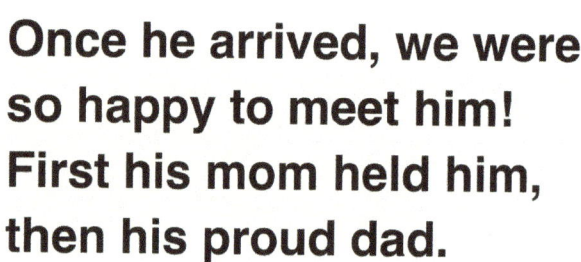

Once he arrived, we were so happy to meet him! First his mom held him, then his proud dad.

Then me, Noonie! We noticed Paul had a lot of hair.

Everyone was so pleased with our new baby
and thankful he had arrived safely.

The next day baby Paul and his mom got to go home from the hospital.

New moms are often very tired after giving birth. They welcome any help they can get from the baby's family and friends.

I wish I could have stayed to help, but it was time to go home. I flew back to Alaska with a heart full of joy at having been there to help welcome a new, tiny person into the family.

Paul was the first of my seven grandchildren and a very important member of the family, as all babies are!

What God says about babies in the womb:

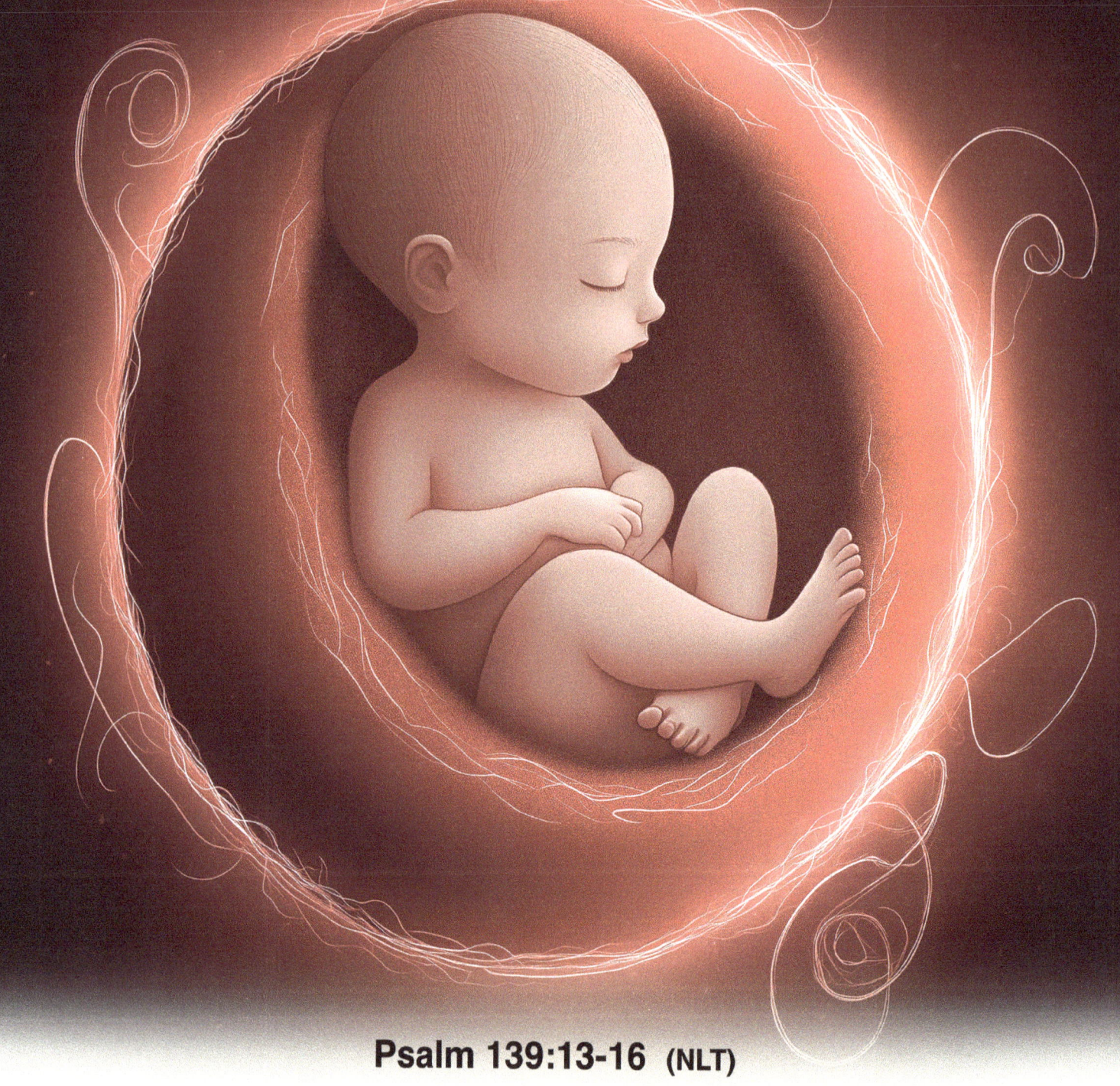

Psalm 139:13-16 (NLT)

"You made all the delicate, inner parts of my body and knit me together in my mother's womb. Thank you for making me so wonderfully complex! Your workmanship is marvelous – how well I know it. You watched me as I was being formed in utter seclusion, as I was woven together in the dark of the womb. You saw me before I was born. Every day of my life was recorded in your book."

What's Your Birth Story?

Ask your family about your birth story:

- **Where were you born?**

- **Were you born early, late, or right on time?**

- **Were you born in the morning, afternoon or night?**

- **Who was there to greet you?**

Relevant Publishers LLC

P.O. Box 505

Sutton, AK 99674

www.relevantpublishers.com

Publisher's Cataloging-In-Publication Data

Names: Ford, Kim, author.
Title: The Big Surprise / written by Kim Ford
Description: Sutton, Alaska : Relevant Publishers, LLC, [2025] | | Interest age level: 004-007. | Summary: "The Big Surprise explores the miracle of birth and teachs children about ultrasounds and babies in the womb. "

Identifiers: ISBN 978-1953263391 (paperback) | ISBN 978-1953263407 (hardback) | ISBN 978-1953263414 (ebook)

Printed in the United States of America

Series List

Book 1...The Big Surprise!
The sanctity of human life, ultrasounds, fetal development, morning sickness, and trimesters explained for children.

Book 2...The Birth That Shook the Earth!
The importance of names and how children get their names, Bible names and unusual names. Includes an unusual birth story and the story of the Biblical Paul and Silas, as well as the gospel.

Book 3...Sharing My Name, Sharing My Mom!
Being named after someone else, sharing your parents with a new baby, bonding with a new family member, differences in our bodies.

Book 4...TWINS!
Morning sickness, finding out about twins, preemies, extended hospital stays for newborns, what it's like to be a twin or a sibling to twins.

Book 5...The Big Reveal Party!
Fun ways families celebrate finding out if a baby is a boy or a girl, meeting a new sibling, breastfeeding introduced, learning to help keep baby siblings safe from choking, and sibling kindness.

Book 6...Born at Home!
Exploring Home births and unusual births, C-sections, midwives, mother's nesting behaviors, contractions and umbilical cords. Includes a story of a modern Christmas baby and the story of the first Christmas.

Book 7...*Title pending*
Being adopted into a family, overcoming jealousy, embracing new people to love.

www.ingramcontent.com/pod-product-compliance
Lightning Source LLC
Chambersburg PA
CBHW041133120626
46547CB00019B/2967

* 9 7 8 1 9 5 3 2 6 3 3 9 1 *